Created This Way

Written & Illustrated By

Sharon L. Stevens

Copyright © 2022

All Rights Reserved

Dedication

To anyone with low self-esteem.

Acknowledgments

I want to acknowledge my awesome husband and close friend, Charles, who has had my back from day one. You are heaven-sent. I'm glad you are in my life.

My precious children, Emmanuel, Tabiyus, Shaterri - I am so glad to be your mother. You three are dear to my heart.

My grandchildren, Ray'Jabeon, My'Angel, Elias, and Brooke'Lynn - Words can't explain the special place that I have for you in my heart.

My mother, Margie - I love you, and I appreciate you for all you have done for me.

All my siblings and Cynthia, a special sister - I truly love you all for making my life complete.

My nieces and nephews, church family - Thank you so much for being part of my life. It's such a blessing, much love.

About the Author

Apostle Sharon Stevens is a retiree from the Department of Social Services. She is a wife, mother of three, and grandmother of four. She is the owner of Christian Way Academy and Sharon's Miracle Hands Company, and the founder of Moving by the Spirit of God Ministries. INC. 1 and 2. Most importantly, she is a pastor who loves to travel, preach and teach the word of God—letting people know that there's hope in God. With him, you can make it!

Apostle Sharon resides in the North Carolina area with her family.

God is perfect, so He created us to be like him. All of God's creations are wonderful, and you are one of them! You can also create things if you desire to make positive changes in your life.

Genesis 1:26 – Then God said, "Let Us make man in Our image, after Our likeness, to rule over the fish of the sea and the birds of the air, and over the cattle and over all the earth, and over every creeping thing that creeps on the earth."

We are happy every day, just knowing that God makes no mistakes in what or who he creates.

Psalm 139:14 – I will praise you, for I am fearfully and wonderfully made. Marvelous are your works, and that my soul knows very well.

Your ears were made to hear sounds; low, medium, or high. What are you hearing right now? Remember, listening is very important.

Your eyes were made to see. God created beautiful sights and landscapes everywhere in the world around you just for you to enjoy. Look at how beautiful are the flowers, trees, grass, all the animals, stars, the moon and the sun. Can you see the clouds? What does the cloud's shape look like to you?

Proverbs 20:12 – The hearing ear and the seeing eye, the Lord has made them both.

Take a look at your nose. I hope you like the way God created it. Remember, you are fearfully and wonderfully made. Your nose is shaped the way it is supposed to be. Breathe in and out. What can you smell?

Genesis 2:7 – And the Lord God formed man of the dust of the ground and breathed into his nostrils (nose) the breath of life, and man became a living soul.

Take a look at your mouth. We can use our mouths for a lot of things. We use our mouths to eat, taste and talk. Are you using words to speak to others with positive words or negative words? It can be used for both good and evil. Ask yourself: Did my words sound pleasing today? Am I speaking with love?

Exodus 4:11 – And the Lord said unto him, Who hath made man's mouth? Or who maketh the dumb, or deaf, or the seeing, or the blind? Have not I the Lord?

Take a look at your hands and notice how our hands are of different sizes. Your hands are created to create. You can build up or break down things with your hand. Most importantly, your hands were made to praise God. How would you like to use your hands?

Psalm 63:4 – Thus will I bless thee while I live: I will lift up my hands in thy name.

Take a look at your feet. They are awesome. They might look different from someone else's, but you are blessed to have them at the end of the day. The left and the right foot work together to get you where you would like to go. What do you think about your feet?

Psalms 119:105 – Thy word is a lamp unto my feet and a light unto my path.

The parts of our body created by God that we have just discussed in this book could not function without the brain (mind). The brain speaks to the ears, eyes, nose, mouth, hands and feet. It's important how we think about things. What we think about is how we feel daily. If we have our minds on sad things, it makes us unhappy. Thinking about joyful things makes us feel happy and excited. Remember, God wants his children to live life peacefully and joyfully. However, sometimes things happen in life that makes us sad.

Colossians 3:2 says, "Set your affection on things above, not on things on the earth."

God gave us our five senses for a reason. We should honor God through our actions and how we use our senses.

Eyes – Sight is manifested through the eyes. They allow us to see colors, light, and dark, allowing us to perceive images and elements. What positive things can you see with your eyes that can change your life?

Ears – Your sense of hearing allows you to listen to the glory of God. Thank God for the special gift of hearing wonderful sounds like birds, music, your friend's laugh. What sound are you hearing clearly right now?

Touch – Our hands detect the temperature of things. Human touch is powerful as it can make us feel both pain and comfort. Jesus used his touch to heal many people, even though he did not need to touch them to heal. May be he used his physical touch to express love and compassion. What are you using your hands for? Are you touching things that will bring you what you need in life to be successful?

Nose – Our sense of smell allows us to detect scents on a surface or in the air. We often do not think about it unless we smell something bad. What can you smell right now right where you are? Do you praise God for sweet smelling flowers or for the aroma of freshly baked brownies?

Tongue – Our taste buds detect a lot of different taste and flavors like bitter, salty, sour, or sweet. Are you tasting something that is good for you or harmful for you? Do you thank God for the wonderful food and flavors in your life?

God has the best for you and he wants you to walk in His blessings. Don't sit there and do nothing about your situation. God has given you the keys to unlock the doors of your blessings.

Matthew 16:19 – And I will give unto the keys of the kingdom of heaven; and whatsoever thou shalt bind on earth shall be bound in heaven; and whatsoever thou shalt loose on earth shall be loosed in heaven.

All things are possible if you believe. Come, it's time to turn your doubts into faith.

Imagine how different life would be if you couldn't taste or see. Teach yourself not to dislike the way God has created you. Learn to appreciate the way he has uniquely created you in His Image and likeness. You are pretty or handsome as you are.

Philippians 4:13 - I can do all things through Christ which strengtheneth me.

Though it is a hard battle in life, trying to figure out who you are, who will accept you, or who will reject you. Just know, that God can change things for you where the darkness has come in through an open door. Speak to yourself about what you want to happen in your life using these words:

I shall have what I desire. What I need in my life is already done.

Romans 8:37 - Nay, in all these things we are more than conquerors through Him who loved us.

Praise Him for you are fearfully and wonderfully made. Marvelous are His works. Walk in the newness of life with Christ.

2 Corinthians 5:17 - Therefore if anyone is in Christ, he is a new creation; the old has gone, the new has come!

We need to use all our senses to empower ourselves as followers of Jesus. God gave us these senses to use in His service. Look up and look forward into your future. Stay positive, touch and speak to people with kindness.

Proverbs 23:7 - For as he thinketh in his heart, so is he. Eat and drink, saith he to thee; but his heart is not with thee.

Even when family and friends don't understand you, remember that God does. Trust him to help you in everything that you do. He can make you a new person. You can be what you desire to be in this world with Jesus in your life.

Remember this, God created us to be like him. If you would like to give your life to the Lord, then today is your day. Follow these steps:

Romans 10:9 - That if thou shalt confess with thy mouth the Lord Jesus, and shalt believe in thine heart that God hath raised him from the dead, thou shalt be saved.

The End.

www.ingramcontent.com/pod-product-compliance
Lightning Source LLC
Chambersburg PA
CBHW060428010526
44118CB00017B/2408